C000128329

Leadership

About the series

Fast Track is a series of short, practical guides designed to get you up to speed on key business and management skills.

Written by experts with many years' experience in the field, each guide gives you instant access to key tips, advice and guidance – information you can put to work straightaway.

First six titles in the series
   Appraisal & Performance Management 1 85835 948 1
   Delegation 1 85835 953 8
   Leadership 1 85835 963 5
   Managing Attendance 1 85835 968 6
   Managing Conflict 1 85835 978 3
   Managing Time 1 85835 958 9

About the Series Editor
Andrew Forrest is Director of Learning and Development at The Industrial Society. He has over 30 years' experience working with and developing people.

Leadership

Ian Lawson

First published in 2001
The Industrial Society
Robert Hyde House
48 Bryanston Square
London W1H 2EA
Telephone: +44 (0)20 7479 2000

© The Industrial Society 2001

ISBN 1 85835 963 5

British Library Cataloguing-in-Publication Data.
A catalogue record for this book is available from the
British Library.

All rights reserved. No part of this publication may be reproduced, stored in a retrieval system or transmitted, in any form or by any means, electronic, mechanical, photocopying, recording and/or otherwise without the prior written permission of the publishers. This book may not be lent, resold, hired out or otherwise disposed of by way of trade in any form, binding or cover other than that in which it is published without prior written consent of the publishers.

Ian Lawson asserts his moral right to be identified as the author of this work.

Printed by: Cromwell Press
Cover image by: Digital Vision
Cover design by: Sign Design
The Industrial Society is a Registered Charity No. 290003

Acknowledgements

I would like to acknowledge the inspiration drawn from working with my colleagues and friends in the Campaign for Leadership, in particular Tayo Richards and Nicollette Shearer for assisting in production of the text, and Andrew Forrest and Susannah Lear for comments around structure, content and ideas.

Contents

Introduction

Management is essentially a science – it is about application, implementation, skills, processes, resources and gradual improvement. *Leadership* is essentially an art – it is about vision, passion, creativity, creating an environment where people can excel and quantum improvement.

In today's complex and competitive world, the need for leadership at all levels – with ideals and approaches that serve both the needs of society and organisations – is vital. The European Foundation for Quality Management recognises 'leadership' as the key enabler spanning all other processes.

There is no shortage of great leaders at all levels – not just directors, managers or politicians, but team members, front line staff and ordinary folk making a difference to their own community.

If there is a perceived shortage it is because our traditions, our systems, our measurements, our own narrow short-termism, but above all *ourselves*, do not let people become the leaders they and we have within.

Many people receive little or no training in leadership despite the fact it is one of the most difficult skills to master.

This guide aims to provide an overview of some of the key aspects of leadership, plus advice on improving your own skills in this vital area.

I have tried to fit the "What do I do as a leader?" into a wider context of the needs of the world of work, drawing on a host of models and research which has resulted in the approach the Campaign for Leadership promotes today – Liberating Leadership. Not everything will be right for everyone, but I encourage you to read through this guide in a spirit of looking for *how* the ideas and concepts could apply, not *if* they could apply.

The book can be in read in about two hours and then serve as a handy reference point for practical steps and tips on a range of key issues.

Why leadership matters

> This chapter covers:
> > Discretionary effort.
> > Leadership and individuals.
> > Leadership and organisations.
> > Leadership and society.

The essential reason why leadership matters is MAKING A DIFFERENCE. As we shall see, the key difference between management and leadership is that leadership is dynamic, it is about change, it is about moving from the *status quo*, whilst management is about perfecting what we already have.

Leadership is about promoting new ideas, gaining better results, striving to implement a policy, living a philosophy and gaining the full engagement of people within an organisation.

A recent survey by pollsters Gallup revealed that the single most frequently cited reason for people leaving their job was the relationship they had with their immediate manager. Put another way some years ago by Jurgen Dunkel, former chief brewer at Tetleys, "80% of my people's effort I can command – the other 20% they choose whether to give to me". In essence, we could call this *discretionary effort*, the part of a person's input at work which distinguishes simple movement from real motivation.

To put this in context consider this statistic. In 2000 in the whole of the UK economy around 1.3 million days were lost due to strike action. During the same period, 184 million days were lost to sickness/absenteeism, over 140 times as many and an equivalent of around 8.5 days per head of the working population.

Now suppose you estimate that some of those days are down to *motivational sickness* (ie the feeling as your alarm goes off on a wet Monday morning that says "I can't be bothered to go to work, I'll call in sick"). Let's say 10%, which is probably pretty conservative. It's fair to say that a large part of that lack of motivation is due to the relationship with the boss and other colleagues in that team.

Just imagine if by leading well we could capture back 10% of those days – what a difference it would make to have an additional 18 million days available to UK plc for increased productivity, attention to customer service or innovation; or not having to spend scare resources (eg covering with supply teachers or agency nurses) in the public sector.

That's a measure of the impact good leadership can have.

Three reasons why

Good leadership matters because of its impact in three areas:

1   Because people matter

People spend most of their waking lives at work. On the down side, this can be a cause of stress, boredom, underachievement, conflict and frustration. On the up side, it can be a significant area for people to build relationships and express their ingenuity, skills, creativity and give them endless opportunities to develop, grow and achieve things they didn't feel possible.

The work of behavioural scientists has demonstrated time and again the importance of fulfilling work and positive relationships at work in gaining high motivation. This is most popularly described through Maslow's 'Hierarchy of Needs', where self-fulfilment is the peak.

Maslow's Hierarchy of Needs

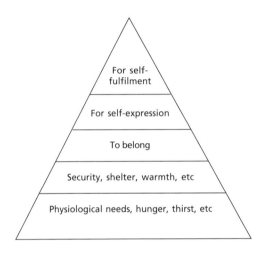

For self-fulfilment

For self-expression

To belong

Security, shelter, warmth, etc

Physiological needs, hunger, thirst, etc

The role of the leader in creating an environment for opportunities and personal development is vital.

2   Because organisations matter

Organisations, whether they be profit-making companies, public services or voluntary organisations, are the bedrock of any society. Leadership gets the results which they need – this may be making a profit and delivering excellent goods and services. It may be providing efficient and caring services in the public sector, upholding the rule of law, educating our young people, etc. **Good results come from good leadership.**

Organisations provide employment, giving meaning to people's lives, wages to support families and individuals, and their success creates profits. All of this feeds into taxes to pay for our public services.

And finally, the culture by which an organisation lives – in treating its staff, customers, suppliers, partners – dramatically affects all those people in the way they view life and interact with others both in and outside of work.

The quality of goods and services is hugely dependent on leadership because leaders give the *why* to what people are doing. As a member of the Probation Board for Northern Ireland said to me, "Leadership gives meaning to processes".

3   *Because society matters*

In all areas of history and society we see leaders making an impact. On the macro level it may be a Gandhi leading the independence movement in India, or it may be the hundreds and thousands of examples at the micro level where leadership has an impact on people's lives.

The integration between society/communities and organisations has always mattered and business leaders have a key role in being 'good citizens' locally, nationally and internationally as appropriate. The resources (not simply money but time, expertise, facilities, knowledge, equipment, etc) which organisations can bring to their communities can be awesome. Some of the world's largest corporations have turnovers well in excess of that of many nations – they have huge influence with government, on the environment, on legislation, etc. For these reasons the state of our society depends on leaders in government, communities and in organisations.

Summary checklist

✓ Focus on the actions you can take to make a difference.

✓ Take accountability for the impact you as a leader may have on people far beyond the narrow confines of achieving the task.

2

What is leadership?

This chapter considers:
> Definitions of leadership.
> Measuring good leadership.
> The 21st century context.

A great many books have been written about leadership, many studies undertaken, great leaders examined and research commissioned. One thing is clear and that is that there is no single or simple answer. There is a huge difference between those people who say "I am right", and those who say "I believe in this approach, and we must continually reflect, learn, observe and be creative in our view on what leadership is". This book is written in the spirit of the latter.

Leadership has been defined in many ways. For example:

"Leadership is about gaining extra-ordinary results from ordinary people", Sir John Harvey-Jones, entrepreneur

"Leadership denotes unleashing energy, building, freeing and growing", Tom Peters, management guru

"Leaders must be close enough to relate to others, but far enough ahead to motivate them", John Maxwell, guru

"Achieving results through people", John Garnett, Director of The Industrial Society, 1962-86.

And we could go on. All of these have merit.

The definition which The Industrial Society believes most usefully reflects the approach needed in the 21st century is drawn from Kouzes and Posner in their book *Credibility*: **"Leadership is a reciprocal relationship between those who choose to lead and those who decide to follow."**

The key words in this are *relationship* – ie leadership is about people not things or systems (management). *Choose* – ie people have to make an active decision to become a leader, it is not achieved merely by virtue of position. An individual must choose to do leaderly things and think and feel in a leaderly way. *Decide* – ie people decide to follow. In other words, people volunteer that discretionary effort or their full engagement in the task required and this is quite distinct from the minimum level of movement or compliance required to do the job.

In short, leadership is not bestowed from above by promotion, it is confirmed from below when the followers see that person as their leader.

Three key areas

Good leadership needs to stand the test of success in three key areas:

1   Achievement

That over time the leader and their team make a difference and achieve goals even though they may also experience failure and may gain success in areas other than they originally intended.

2   The journey

Results are not the only thing that matters. The method, the *how*, the journey is an equally important consideration for leaders. Have we achieved success in an ethical way? Have we been true to our people and our principles? What have we learned from our efforts?

3   *Legacy*

In my view a leader should be judged as much on events and scenarios one, two, three, four even five years after they have gone than on the successes during and at the end of their time. Have changes lasted? Have they proved beneficial? Have the leaders' successors taken things forward or has the whole enterprise crumbled?

A new paradigm? New role models?

Often when we ask people to think of leaders we get examples who are historical, male, usually military or political. In a great many cases these examples do not meet the three criteria set out above. This is not to say that these people were not great leaders, but is to say that they were people of their time and circumstances. It is likely that our new role models will come as much from imagining a new future as from examining great figures from the past.

The 21st century context – four key aspects

1   *Change*

The scale and pace of change is now so dramatic that individuals and organisations have little idea what the medium term or even short term may hold. Essentially, leadership promotes and harnesses change. Management is about implementation and application. Everybody's job, particularly managers, is increasingly about change, therefore the leadership content is increasing.

2   Expectations

Expectations of people are hugely more sophisticated and discerning. Mobility, skills shortages and a refreshing lack of deference to the 'establishment' mean leaders have to win people's hearts *and* minds. The failure of many business leaders and politicians to behave with integrity and real vision is more sharply in focus (thanks often to the media) than ever before. People expect and deserve better.

3   Legislation

Legislation around Human Rights, Health & Safety, Equal Opportunities, the environment, etc are forcing organisations to consider the holistic results of their actions both short and long term.

4   Globalisation

The globalisation of competition, markets, instant worldwide communication and 'mobility' of labour have placed huge demands on companies to be more efficient and effective. The plain truth is that in nearly all cases the competitive advantage lying in organisations rests only with its people.

Summary checklist

✓ Recognise that leadership has no simple formula for success. Be open to the range of opinions and make your own choices.

✓ Look beyond short-term task achievement to set your own measures for success.

3

Approaches to leadership

This chapter offers an overview of key
leadership approaches:
> Action Centred Leadership.
> Situational Leadership.
> Emotional Intelligence.
> Transactional/Transformational Leadership.
> Liberating Leadership.

Action Centred Leadership (ACL)

One of the simplest but most effective leadership models has been the ACL approach developed by John Adair and The Industrial Society in the late 1960s.

The basis of this approach is that a leader must concentrate on actions in order to be successful. Not only is this vital in order for things to happen, but it is also of huge benefit in individual learning and organisational leadership training. This is because it puts the focus on what people *do* not on their personal qualities. This means we can observe others, clearly identify actions that leaders need to *do* (eg brief the team, hold 'one-to-ones' [regular individual reviews], set targets, etc). It is practical, easy to replicate and simple and, as Einstein said, "Things should be as simple as possible but no simpler".

Any successful leader should be aware of the ACL model as a foundation for the areas to take action.

These fall into three key areas:

- Actions to achieve the task
- Actions to build the team
- Actions to develop individuals.

This is best expressed by the well-known ACL model of the three circles. This has been widely adopted in every area of the world of work.

The ACL model

Clearly, leaders have a need to achieve the task as this is why the team and organisation exist. However, too much attention to this one circle will lead to a reduction in effort from the team and individuals. If a manager pays no account of their team's needs as people then the team will do what is required but no more, and ultimately the task will not be achieved to the levels possible. A typical model of an overly task-focused leader would look like this:

The task-focused leader

The work environment of the overly task-focused leader is often characterised by moderate or low achievement, low morale and high turnover of staff. In a crisis people can live with this but not for a sustained period of time.

The team-focused leader

Similarly, the team-building circle is vital. The group synergy of a team who work well together can produce a great working environment and great results. Lots of ideas, mutual support and improved performance can result. But if the team circle is consistently out of kilter then individuals can feel neglected and the need to get the job done can be overlooked. Typically, this sort of leader tries to avoid individual conflicts and aims to keep the team happy, sometimes at the expense of results. In the long run, of course, things don't work out as people don't respond or feel motivated working in a team which consistently fails.

The individual-focused leader

In the individual circle, attention is paid more specifically to personal skills and needs in the job. We are all different, and different approaches, levels of support or briefing and attention to non-work issues mean that this circle is important. Again, distorted amounts of time and attention directed to one person (classically either a favourite or a troublesome team member) will have a negative effect both on the team and the achievement of the task because other team members will feel neglected.

Identifying the processes and actions required means combining the areas of the three circles with the following well-established five stage action cycle:

- Define objectives
- Plan
- Brief
- Monitor/Support
- Evaluate.

Viewed as a cycle these areas must be visited and revisited by the leader in both small and large tasks.

The five stage action circle

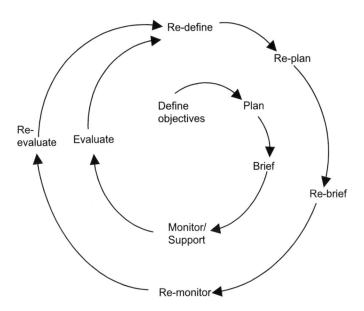

By mapping together the things which need to be done, and the area of team action where they take place, it is easy to build up a leadership framework (*see overleaf*).

A leadership framework

Key actions		Task	Team	Individual
Define objectives		Identify tasks and constraints	Hold team meetings Share commitment	Clarify objectives Gain acceptance
Plan	Gather information	Consider options Check resources	Consult Develop suggestions	Encourage ideas Assess skills
	Decide	Priorities Time-scales Standards	Structure	Allocate jobs Delegate Set targets
Brief		Clarify objectives Describe plan	Explain decisions Answer questions Check understanding	Listen Enthuse
Monitor/Support		Assess progress Maintain standards	Co-ordinate Reconcile conflict	Advise/Assist/ Reassure/Counsel Discipline
			Recognise effort	
Evaluate		Summarise Review objectives Re-plan if necessary	Recognise and gain from success Learn from mistakes	Appraise performance
			Guide and train	Give praise

By doing one becomes

The final principle in ACL is that by observing the actions/behaviours required, and practising them, you will become a better leader. By briefing you will communicate better and come to be seen as the leader, by setting targets you will improve your ability to do this and so forth.

ACL has been widely adapted by organisations in all areas of work and at all levels. It is a superb foundation for understanding how to improve leadership abilities.

Situational Leadership

There have been two main approaches to Situational Leadership. The first – widely practised but not laid down in textbooks – is that of the technically most competent person being put in a leadership role. This is still commonplace – typically the best fitter becomes the supervisor or the best salesperson becomes the sales manager. As the skills required for leading people have little to do with technical competence, organisations are littered with people promoted into positions they are ill-suited to and in which they under-perform. This is often compounded by the lack of any adequate training or coaching in the new aspects of their role.

The second approach to Situational Leadership is drawn from the Hersey and Blanchard model (1977) that leaders need to be aware of the relationship between 'people' behaviour (encouragement, support, etc) and 'task' behaviour (structure, direction). People are at different stages and therefore require a different style.

The classic flow is as follows:

Telling ⟶ Selling ⟶ Participating ⟶ Delegating
(Structuring (Coaching (Encouraging (Letting go)
style) style) style)

This approach has strength in that it encourages leaders to take account of the environment in which they work, and the people they work with, and act accordingly. The difficulty lies in quickly and accurately assessing the correct approach and in not confusing the workforce by constantly changing how the leader operates.

Emotional Intelligence

Daniel Goleman's influential book *Emotional Intelligence* has highlighted the need for leaders to pay heed to their feelings and instincts, and those of others. In other words, 'EQ' is as important, indeed more powerful in leadership terms, than 'IQ'.

Essentially, Goleman establishes five domains to emotional intelligence:

- Recognising one's own emotions
- Managing one's own emotions
- Motivating ourselves
- Recognising emotions in others
- Managing relationships and motivating others.

Research conducted by The Industrial Society has demonstrated that a climate of trusting relationships underpins any successful leader. Much of this will derive from the elements established above.

Transactional/Transformational Leadership

Transactional Leadership is based around a leader having clear goals and objectives, and then gaining employees 'buy in' through good communication and motivational skills. Motivational factors could include pay, praise, better jobs, listening, etc; or management by exception, ie applying corrective action when performance is inadequate. Of course, both approaches can be used by the same leader.

Transformational Leadership implies a real engagement between leader and 'follower'. The leader's vision is achieved by raising individuals' awareness about the vision and associated issues and concentrating on their growth and development.

Liberating Leadership

The Industrial Society has been campaigning for good leadership for around 30 years. In the second half of the 1990's we decided to undertake a complete review of our approach to leadership, underpinned by a major piece of research.

Huge changes had occurred in the workplace, with flatter structures, increased flexible working, breakdown of hierarchies and a continued move towards less formality. The demands placed upon organisations for greater productivity, higher quality, better customer service and increased efficiency were huge. Competition, globalisation and downsizing were all watchwords.

Our research included desk research, focus groups and large-scale survey work.

Discussions with senior business people identified key success factors for the organisations of the future:

- Leaders who will make the right 'space' for people to perform well without having to be watched over.

- Flat structures where people can be trusted to work with minimal supervision.

- A wide range of people to be able to 'take a lead' and see through a project, step into a leadership role when necessary and consistently behave in a responsible way.

- A culture where people can be responsive to customer demands and agile in the face of changing technology.

Key to this survey of people at work was two things:

1 Respondents were asked to think of a leader they had personal experience of and describe in a couple of sentences a situation where they had benefited from that person's good leadership.

2 Based upon the above situation the respondents then ranked a number of characteristics/behaviours associated with effective leadership.

The results showed very clearly that the key theme for successful leadership was the establishment of *trusting relationships*. That this was derived by judging the 'visible' behaviours of the leader and that these derived from the leader's belief system.

Quoted, real-life examples from this research are given in **bold italics** during the following chapters to illustrate some of the key themes.

Three key components were identified within this belief system:

1   Self-belief

Staff need to be able to trust their manager to take decisions which will ensure the team's/department's/organisation's success. The leader's track record of results and how they have been achieved (ie *with* staff, *not* at their expense) is therefore important. Despite a good track record, however, people will not have confidence in leaders who do not appear to have confidence in themselves. Leaders must demonstrate their self-belief by their daily behaviour. It is particularly important to be unruffled when under pressure. Staff are unlikely to trust a manager who is seen to panic in a crisis.

2   Integrity and fairness

Our research findings place great emphasis on the need for leaders to be truthful. Failure to do so rapidly creates a climate where everything is questioned. In times of rapid change this may involve being open to the fact that the leader and the organisation may not know all the answers, what lies ahead or why it may be necessary to keep certain information confidential (eg for legal, commercial or personal reasons).

Staff expect leaders to give credit where credit is due and put their staff's interests on the same level as their own.

3   Beliefs about others

Trust is mutual. People are unlikely to trust a manager who clearly does not trust them. Good leaders see the good in others and give people the benefit of the doubt, without being naïve. They genuinely want others to succeed.

These beliefs could be maintained in the behaviour of the leader – for example, if you didn't really believe in developing people this would show up, say, in how you conducted appraisals. Such leaders would be likely to postpone appraisals at short notice, do minimal preparation, be hostile to feedback, etc. In other words, over time it would be very hard for a leader not to betray their inner beliefs through their behaviour.

To create a constructive and practical approach the Society developed **Liberating Leadership**.

Note the word Liberating – not empowered. Empowerment, whilst an important step on the way to liberation, suggests a significant element of top-down process. If the leader can empower, so they can *dis*empower. In creating a climate where people are liberated, the leader unleashes what is within people – and once that particular genie is out of the bottle, there is no going back…

To support the application of the broader philosophy we developed an equation, a model and a mnemonic with 38 behaviours.

The leadership equation

Leadership recognition =

| **Leadership skills and practices** | + | **Aligned beliefs** | + | **Trusting relationships** |

In other words, we will actually see good leadership when these things come together – good skills and behaviours (what we see) underpinned by an aligned set of beliefs (our being) and a climate of trusting relationships.

The Leader-Ship model

For some people it is easier to see things as shapes or models. For this, we developed the 'Leader-Ship'.

In this model there are two broad areas:

1 Behaviours which are skills, competencies and practices

2 Behaviours which build trust.

The first category of behaviours is easy to see – listening, coaching, target setting, decision-taking, etc. A leader would demonstrate these within a relatively short time.

The second category takes more time. People will only build up trust over a period, based on such things as the leader keeping their word, looking out for others' interests as well as their own, etc.

Both are formed by underlying beliefs, which is why this is represented by the hull *below* the water line.

The keel represents the climate of trust which a Liberating Leader must engender to succeed.

The 'LEADER' mnemonic

'LEADER' builds a useful mnemonic. The key message is that leaders need to develop all six activities listed below in order to succeed.

	Liberate	by freeing those closest to the job to take their own decisions
	Encourage	staff and support them when necessary
	Achieve	the purpose for which the team exists
	Develop	people and teams
set an	**E**xample	through their own behaviour
build	**Relationships**	on trust

The mnemonic LEADER starts with L for Liberates. This is most appropriate as this single word encapsulates the very essence of this philosophy of leadership.

Summary checklist

✓ Understand the different approaches to leadership and see *how* you can apply them through real-time experimentation.

Liberates

This chapter advises on:
> Avoiding blame cultures.
> Listening and developing ideas.
> Empowering staff.

Liberates indicates release – the release of the potential, imagination, creativity, commitment and skills which are in all of us. 'Liberates' is about creating an environment where other people can shine.

Of course, there is a huge difference between Liberation and Abdication. The latter occurs when the leader simply leaves people to get on with it, with inadequate framing, direction, support or guidance. The leader can never absolve themselves of the overall responsibility for their people and on occasions their lack of success. Similarly, the leader should feel able to take considerable credit if things go well, even if their active part may seem to have been small.

Andrew Carnegie is said to have declared that the greatest leadership tip he could give was to "surround yourself with people who are better than yourself". This may feel personally uncomfortable, but it is a sure-fire way to succeed.

Moving from a traditional culture to a liberated one is not easy – nor can it happen instantaneously or to the same degree or at the same speed for all team members. One analogy is to consider a box containing fleas. As the fleas jump around so they will hit the sides – after a while, even with their tiny brains, fleas learn the constraints of the box and jump within it. As an analogy for many organisations it is apt; the fleas represent the staff – full of energy and free-spirited – the box represents the constraints, the procedures/systems and lack of authority which hems in many people at work.

Now imagine you remove the box. Two things happen – either the fleas continue to jump within the same constraints (as they are now conditioned to do so) or the more adventurous ones leap off in all directions and are never seen again. The equivalent is staff continuing to behave in the same old way, or staff 'abusing' their freedom by doing whatever they like.

So how can real Liberation be accompanied by some consistency and direction? This is a critical point – how to create a CHAORDIC organisation/team? To some degree, it is the coming together of leadership (chaos) and management (order), but the most powerful element is a shared direction and a shared set of values or principles and agreed standards to work to. The leader sets these and individuals need to have an alignment with them. They can then perform to high levels within the required general framework.

This is the scenario described by Warren Bennis as "herding cats".

Key behaviours/attributes

'Liberate' within the mnemonic is made up of six behaviours/attributes. These are:

- Not blaming your staff for their mistakes
- Encouraging people closest to the job to take their own decisions
- Listening to staff
- Encouraging full and open communication

- Operating systems based on trust not suspicion
- Encouraging staff to develop new ideas.

Not blaming your staff for their mistakes

There are few organisations that proclaim they *have* a blame culture; many openly state they are in or trying to *move* towards a no-blame culture. But regrettably most still operate in a blame-seeking way. Now, a no-blame culture does not mean lack of accountability *or* lack of consequences if things go wrong or performance is not up to the mark. Neither does it excuse mistakes which are repeated, sloppy, endanger life or limb, or are wilful.

We all make mistakes, mistakes will always be made, so it is better to have a culture which encourages their early identification and rectification and learns from the scenario rather than one in which people try to cover mistakes up. In which case mistakes will still happen, they will just be harder to see and do more damage.

There is a story of a senior marketing manager charged with the launch of a major new product – the launch cost $1 million but was a complete flop. The manager felt sure the CEO would ask for his head – sure enough, within a few days, he was summoned to the CEO's office. Expecting the worst he wrote out his resignation letter and handed it to the CEO – "What's this?", the CEO said. "It's my resignation", the manager replied, "I felt sure that after such a costly mistake you would want my resignation". "Not a bit of it", replied the CEO, "I've just invested $1 million in your training!"

Mistakes are inevitable and we must treat them as valuable opportunities to learn for the future. When working on developing the light bulb, Thomas Edison and his assistant failed *yet* again. His assistant said, "We have failed 1,000 times – let's give up". Edison replied, "Not at all, we now know of 1,000 different ways in which it will *not* work".

Encouraging people closest to the job to take their own decisions

The opposite of this can be seen in many traditional organisations where decisions go through numerous layers in a hierarchical pyramid. In some cases a culture of liberation has been forced upon people because of a rapidly imposed reduction in middle management layers. If this approach is viewed from a more positive angle – as a consequence of an enriching culture rather than simply cost savings – it promotes an entirely different approach to transition, training and development, resourcing, authenticity, measures and rewards.

People have huge responsibilities outside of their jobs, which they often manage exceedingly well. People have families and financial responsibilities, plan holidays, purchase houses, etc. Tom Peters says that in any group of staff, when you look at what they do outside of work, you will find such undertakings as lay preacher, treasurer of the football club, etc, etc.

The down side to the traditional hierarchical approach, beyond its slowness, is its inability to respond to customer needs. I was recently at Heathrow Airport waiting for a colleague from the US whose plane was late. To kill time I decided to have a snack at one of the airport cafés. I asked for an omelette plus a round of bread and butter. The server replied that they had no bread and butter, only toast. Desperately trying to repress the irony and sarcasm welling up inside me, I asked for an omelette, some butter and a round of uncooked toast! Success, but surely the server should have felt empowered to work that one out?

Conversely, on a visit to North West Trains a couple of years back, I learnt that they had agreed a system to allow local ticket officers to issue refunds for incorrect tickets, or ones not used due to the railway's failure, up to an agreed amount of money. So much better than the customer having to write off to customer relations at headquarters.

A good indicator of how far a leader pushes decision taking down the line is whether they feel uncomfortable. Ben Thompson McCausland (former CEO, National & Provincial Building Society) says you should "delegate until it hurts!"

"Our manager instructs the team as to what needs doing but gives the team autonomy as to how to do it. She is available at all times for guidance and support and uses a participative style of leadership to make decisions that affect the team".

Listening to your staff

To be a great listener is key to great leadership. Listening not only gives us many, many more good ideas – it also motivates our staff, because to be listened to is to be valued.

Stephen Covey says, "Seek first to understand, then to be understood".

This insightful comment recognises the importance of "listening to understand" as opposed to:

- Listening to agree
- Listening to disagree
- Listening for what we have already heard
- Listening for someone to be wrong
- Listening to 'look good'
- Listening to interrupt
- Listening to say what we want to say, etc.

In listening to understand, we need to recognise all the clutter and conversations in our minds – much of which we cannot avoid. A combination of our social conditioning, experiences, the environment we are in, the topic, our relationship with the speaker, plus our own abstract thoughts (anything from great work ideas to what you're having for dinner), all act to distract us from really active listening.

Recognising this danger is a big step towards active listening. The other key is to listen for *how* rather than *if* what the speaker says could work for us in some way. If we can truly do this then we can really see where they are coming from and then, and only then, decide what we wish to take on board.

Tips to improve listening abilities include:

- Inviting comment
- Picking a conducive time and environment
- Listening for what is *not* said as well as what is said
- Listening for emotions as well as facts
- Using eye contact, body language and supportive comments to encourage the speaker
- Focusing on the message rather than the delivery
- Asking questions for clarification
- Reflecting and summarising our understanding
- Building on their thought with our own questions/ suggestions.

Encouraging full and open communication

Is it ever possible to have full, open and honest communication? Probably not, and it could be taken to ridiculous degrees. However, we are talking about an environment, an overall 'soup' if you like, where people know about direction, possibilities, problems, the reasons for decisions and basically trust that the organisation and its leaders are being open. The key is, do people feel communication is *authentic*?

There are times when you, as a leader, should not be open – for legal reasons, on issues of personal confidentiality, sensitive business issues, etc. But these constraints can be explained.

But by and large it is better to be transparent because without it people make up their own version of events – frequently negative – and the truth normally gets out anyway.

Where things cannot be shared, it is better to be upfront and explain why.

Key to good communication is the big picture and context. Establishing the climate does not come quickly. Indeed, Admiral Sir Raymond Lygo (Chairman, TNT) talks of the "100 tellings", ie the need to keep repeating consistent messages via different media to get them to stick. Values and purpose are particularly important – values are essentially about *how* we go about things and how we deal with each other, customers, suppliers, etc while purpose (a vision) is about *why* we are putting all this effort in. People can do almost any amount of 'what' if they have enough 'why'.

Full communication involves all potential media – electronic mail, videos, presentations, one-to-ones, appraisals, walking the job, etc. But leaders forget the importance of face to face at their peril. The studies of Albert Meherabien demonstrated that in gaining understanding (the precursor to 'buy in') non-verbal communication rated 55% against 38% for voice tone, and only 7% for the actual words. We must therefore craft the delivery for conviction as well as the words for impact.

Operating systems based on trust not suspicion

The most important finding from our leadership research was that people were inspired by leaders who created *trusting relationships*.

When we look at the typical systems in many organisations it is difficult to square them with trusting people. For example:

- Clocking in
- Expenditure authorisation levels for different levels of staff

- The need for minor expenses to be signed off.

In HM Customs, senior managers submit their own expenses rather than having them signed off by their manager. Considering the huge spans of control and expenditure these people have, it does seem sensible within the constraints of what are allowable expenses to trust them with a few hundred pounds – and in any case, all such systems are (rightly) subjected to occasional audit.

Have a look at your own systems, what messages do they send out to your staff?

Encouraging your staff to develop new ideas

One of the most exciting and motivating situations for a member of staff is to have ideas requested, listened to and then implemented. Better still, the individual is able to see through their ideas themselves. There is seldom a more powerful champion than the author of an idea.

The speed of change and the degree of detail and specialism required at all levels means it is wholly inappropriate for the leader to expect to have to come up with all or most of the team's ideas.

The areas where staff can contribute most are 'off the wall' ideas, generated by pilots, brainstorming and inspiration, and completely new ideas, generated by imagining the future as we wish it to be.

There is tremendous power in creating a future as we would wish it and then working backwards for the opportunities and ideas to get there. If people can be shown the possibilities of thinking this way, who knows what will flow from it?

By celebrating success, quick wins and acknowledging the value of those that don't work, leaders will create a climate where people go ahead and do or try rather than sit and wait for approval or go through the stifling effort of committee management.

Summary checklist

✓ Adapt behaviours which assume there are talents and ideas within your people waiting to be tapped.

✓ Push accountability, authority and resources as far as possible to the people at the front line.

✓ Check internal policies and systems for congruence with a liberated culture.

Encourages and supports

This chapter offers advice on:
> Supporting your staff.
> Watching for stress.
> Demonstrating faith in people.

Key behaviours/attributes

This area covers the following attributes:

- Accepting responsibility for the actions of your staff

- Giving praise where it's due

- Recognising and acting to minimise other people's stress

- Supporting your staff when they need it

- Regularly meeting with individuals to clarify direction

- Making people feel important and showing that you have faith in them.

Accepting responsibility for the actions of your staff

Accepting responsibility is hugely important in terms of building trust with your team and colleagues. It is very tempting, very easy and very short-sighted for a leader to distance themselves if a staff member makes an error or is underperforming. The leader is not personally accountable for the incident or trend *per se* – but they *are* responsible possibly for why it happened (if the staff member was inadequately trained or briefed, pushed beyond their limits, misled, etc); and they certainly are responsible and accountable for what action results. This could be learning from the experience, retraining, development, giving the task to someone else, discipline or any number of other options.

The word 'WE' becomes very important when a leader talks with a team member as does a 'focus' on the future in terms of action.

Of course, this assumes that taking responsibility can feel negative – in fact most people do a good job most of the time, many an exceptional job some of the time and a few an exceptional job most or all of the time. The leader should also feel responsible for this as they have created a climate in which it happens.

"A manager sacrificed his own credibility to protect a member of his staff who had seriously misjudged a situation. The manager desperately proceeded to provide the necessary support to ensure it didn't happen again, saving a career and maintaining a loyal employee whose efforts over time would more than repay the initial losses".

Giving praise where it's due

How often do you hear people complain that "management never say thank you"? Too often? Perhaps it is human nature... The story is told of a couple, one of whom decided to surprise their partner by painting the bedroom. All went well except they missed one tiny corner. When their partner saw the room this was what they noticed, not the 98% which was right.

Similarly, if you look at these numbers, what do you see?

1+1=2	4+4=9	*Most of us see that 4+4=9 is*
2+2=4	5+5=10	*inaccurate not that the other*
3+3=6	6+6=12	*five equations are correct.*

The first lesson in praise is to "catch people doing things right". Another useful method is to praise people to somebody else, another manager for example, and copy them in on the letter or e-mail.

It is important to praise genuinely for output or effort above the norm, or new ideas, or simply a magic moment or behaviour trait you wish to reinforce. However, don't overdo it as it appears insincere and loses all value. Remember that senior people tend to get praised even less frequently and there is no shame in praising *your* boss if they have done something really well.

Recognising and acting to minimise other people's stress

It is calculated that stress costs the UK economy many millions of pounds every year. When you add the inconvenience, disruption and real damage that can be done at work and in people's lives by stress, you begin to get a sense of its importance. People take it for granted that senior managers suffer from stress, however, studies in the automotive industry show that working on the production line with its seeming relentless pressure was as, if not more, stressful and even led to occupational sabotage in order to get a break.

Typical symptoms of stress for yourself and others include:

- Emotional outbursts
- Irregular attendance
- Irritability
- Simple errors
- Agitated manner
- Taking work home

- Customer complaints
- Tiredness
- Inability to make decisions.

Often this comes from people having a combination of high challenge but low support:

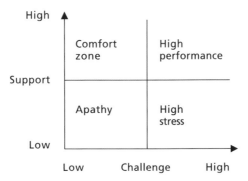

Continued high stress leads to **burn out** – the opposite, continued apathy, can lead to **rust out**.

People can be helped by reviewing workloads and methods, diary management, assertiveness training, time off, professional help and many more methods. Personally, as a leader, I have found the most useful techniques to be:

- Doing less to achieve more (ie devoting effort to priorities – low priorities go away, sort themselves or become high priorities).

- Not allowing things outside our control to wind us up (especially being late because of travel!) – this is a state of mind. I mean *really*, will it matter in a week or so's time?

It is important for leaders to care for and be *seen* to care for their staff, both on a personal level and because of the potential effect on the operation.

Supporting your staff when they need it

This attribute links very closely with the one about stress. It is a vital part of building trust within the team and of realising and maintaining high performance.

Leaders need to be aware of a number of different levels at which to operate. It may become obvious that people need support when things start to go wrong (see stress signs list), when performance is poor or because you hear things from other colleagues.

Most of us are not paid to be, not do we have the qualifications to be, an effective agony aunt or counsellor. But the simple act of asking and listening is often a huge step forward in helping somebody.

If it is a domestic issue, it will mainly be about listening or suggesting professional advice. Beware if you are a man – our tendency is to want to 'fix things' when women often wish to talk, share and be listened to.

If the problem is work based and about relationships, the most effective way forward is normally to get the people concerned to talk, perhaps engaging third party facilitation if required.

Performance issues are sometimes easier to diagnose and often there is greater clarity on the action required. Regular review meetings will be a great benefit to both parties, providing an early opportunity to identify issues and 'nip them in the bud'.

"A recently promoted member of staff was finding it difficult to adjust to her new role and the demands that were being made on her. Her supervisor picked up on this immediately and set about resolving the situation, quickly and without highlighting the problem to other members of staff".

Regularly meeting with individuals to clarify direction

With most people's busyness at work, it is crucial to set aside time for one-to-one reviews. These need not take a great deal of time. The purpose is to check on work progress, set new priorities/targets, identify and discuss any issues and check and build on the relationship between leader and team member.

It is rather like checking whilst sailing a yacht that you are still heading for the right destination rather than leaving it until you arrive to find out whether you got there!

Meeting face to face and following a format of areas to consider (often with a brief follow-up note) is hugely useful in maintaining an individual's sense of value and importance. It allows for rapid support, corrective action and the opportunity to build on success.

Making people feel important and showing you have faith in them

There are a number of ways to do this – the most difficult, but also the most valuable, are giving time to people and listening to them. Leaders often spend far too much time *doing* rather than *leading*. It is easy for staff to feel neglected even if this is not your intent. This is best overcome by good diary control, drills for one-to-ones and meetings, and a strong sense of priorities. Remember, leadership is the people part of management and will tend to be about the 'soft' areas of behaviour or performance. Good soft skills can get great hard results.

Social gatherings, impromptu celebrations for success, marking people's birthdays, personalised thank you notes to people – all of these make people feel important and are well worth the time invested in them.

Showing faith in people is principally about what you let them do at work. This may be delegating part of your job, letting them run with a new idea, giving them more responsibility, giving them the lead role in an important presentation, etc. It may also be about how you consult them – involving them and gaining their views on key projects or on how to handle a difficult situation with a customer or colleague.

In essence, no matter what you say it will be your behaviour and actions which speak to people most powerfully in this area.

Summary checklist

✓ Ensure regular one-to-one contact is in place to give direction and support.

✓ Take opportunities publicly to praise staff and look to reinforce the things they are doing well.

✓ Build in time for formal and informal contact to check progress and demonstrate that people's contributions matter.

6

Achieves purpose

This chapter offers advice on:
> Achieving results.
> Target setting.
> Taking tough decisions.
> Getting out of the comfort zone.

In the Liberating Leadership approach, there is a lot more at stake than simply 'achieving purpose'.

Principally:

- How can purpose be achieved? (The journey is important, not just the destination)

- Could more have been achieved? (Has the leader *really* added value?)

- What is the legacy?

This is not to say that 'achieving purpose' – getting results – is not important or not as important. Simply that the results we need to consider are a lot broader *and* deeper than simply achieving a task. It clearly still remains important for leaders to get results for the success of the organisation and the self-esteem of the team.

Key behaviours/attributes

The seven attributes in this part of the mnemonic are:

- Achieving results
- Agreeing demanding targets with individuals or teams
- Consulting those affected before making decisions
- Being willing to take unpopular decisions in order to move forward
- Seeking out future challenges and opportunities
- Regularly communicating an inspiring view of the future
- Constantly seeking to improve the way things are done.

Achieving results

When it comes to achieving results we are talking on two levels with Liberating Leadership. First, the need for the leader and team to be successful in the achievement of the routine tasks to the high standards set. Secondly, and more importantly, to be gaining quantum leaps in their results. For most organisations, incremental change is no longer adequate. This is not to say that it is about working harder or necessarily producing more, but it is about moving into new areas, using new methods and inventing completely new ways of operating.

The role of the leader is to create a new paradigm within which people operate. This allows a totally new set of possibilities to emerge. When people are aware of these new possibilities they begin to see opportunities which always existed but only become apparent because they are seeing the world differently.

Then, and only then, can leaders and teams begin to plan by allocating clear accountabilities, outcomes and actions. This leads to the new levels of results required. Current thinking tends towards leaping into action – being busy is seen as a good thing – but while it does get results it rarely achieves what could be possible. Results need to hit the stakeholders in all areas, not simply a narrow, short-term bottom line.

Agreeing demanding targets with individuals or teams

Targets and measures are really important to achieve success, for motivation and a sense of accomplishment, and to focus resources on key priorities. The main questions which you as an individual need to address are:

- What is my purpose?
- What are my key result areas?
- What ongoing levels of performance/behaviours are expected from me? (Standards)
- What additional priorities must I focus on? (Targets)
- How will I know whether I am successful?

Targets can be to address a level of low performance, to raise performance beyond current standards or to develop a completely new area. It is always best to involve teams and individuals in setting targets in order to gain their input and ideas as well as their engagement (ie living it not just talking the talk). People will normally respond better to this approach than having targets imposed. This does not negate the role of the leader in making the final decision on what is required. It can often be the case that the leader needs people to do more than they believe they can do.

Must targets be agreed? Ideally, yes but the reality is that this may not always be possible. If it isn't possible, then it is vital to gain *alignment* ("I will go all out for it even if I have reservations") – this can be achieved if people understand the *why* behind the decision and have had the opportunity to be listened to. With alignment it is still possible to gain engagement.

> *"Our manager created an excellent team spirit and motivated each of the team to give their best. He did this by setting clear objectives, giving clear individual responsibility and providing support when difficulties arose".*

Consulting those affected before making decisions

The International Labour Organisation's definition of consultation is "management *genuinely* seeking the views of the workforce *before* decisions are taken which affect them".

A common refrain at work is "nobody ever asks us". Too often management not only think they have the right answers but also fail to appreciate the extent to which their staff actually want to help.

Consultation naturally garners many ideas which would not have been dreamt of, but it also gains vital insights into people's thinking, feelings and priorities. Decisions which are difficult to implement can be made easier for all concerned when this information is gleaned. Consultation can vary from the blank sheet of paper approach, eg "How should the office look after we move?", to the more specific setting out of proposals.

We ignore consultation, or do it badly, at our peril – I well remember re-designing the team's office many years ago and consulting in detail with the dozen or so team members involved. We produced plans, moved around bits of paper representing people and furniture, agreed principles. Everything was fine apart from the one person (on a lengthy holiday) who missed the process and totally disagreed with her new location; as much energy was spent trying to find a win-win solution with her as on the original exercise!

Being willing to take unpopular decisions in order to move forward

As The Industrial Society profiles more and more managers on our leadership programmes, we are able to amass some very interesting information. (Respondents now run well over the 10,000 mark.) This particular behaviour is one where managers are frequently marked relatively low.

Taking difficult decisions may be shied away from, or done in a way which tries to conceal those aspects likely to be unpopular.

It may be a necessary decision but one likely to be unpopular with the team, or it may be dealing with members of the team whose performance or behaviour is unacceptable.

People like to know where they stand and would prefer straight talk, even if it is unpalatable to them. To do otherwise is not to show respect.

In cases of poor performance or behaviour, it is important to act swiftly – both for morale and fairness.

For leaders the key principle is to remember that gaining and holding people's respect is more valuable than trying to be popular; the latter approach in itself frequently backfires and leads to a lack of achievement.

Seeking out future challenges and opportunities

This is a vital area. The only thing we know for sure about the future is that it is likely to be very different from the present.

Most major organisations which existed at the turn of the 20th century no longer exist. Who would have thought it possible that Pan Am or Barings would have floundered? Or that we would have the current truly international ownership and alliances within the automotive industry? It is really quite hard to keep track of who owns whom.

A major concern for leaders and teams here is to create an

atmosphere where people are 'comfortable being uncomfortable', by which I mean being used to operating outside of their comfort zone. Each time we are able to do this we grow as people. Every time we move out of the shaded area (see diagram below) – whether or not we 'succeed' – we *learn* and by so doing increase the size of that area and our own portfolio as individuals.

"My manager succeeds by setting clear objectives, reviewing the project at regular intervals, giving assistance whenever required but not taking control of my individual task".

Regularly communicating an inspiring view of the future

Vision gives us our purpose, a framework for operating. It provides the *why* as well as the *what* for people at work.

Imagine there are three people laying bricks on top of one another and you ask what they are doing – three answers come back:

1   "I'm laying bricks on top of one another".

2   "I'm building a wall".

3   "I'm helping to build a cathedral".

It was Voltaire who said "To unite men and women we have to give them cathedrals to build". What is your/your team's cathedral?

The leader's role here is far beyond setting the vision, it is getting people to see that they make a contribution to it *and* live it.

Organisational visions may be broken down into team or individual ones. To really grasp the imagination it is best if a vision can be expressed succinctly – not several pages long, probably not more than seven words.

The Industrial Society's vision is "Campaigning to improve working life"; Federal Express's is "The world on time".

People will march for a sentence, but they won't march for a paragraph because they can't remember it! A vision will inspire, challenge and allow measures to be set to gauge how well we are progressing.

Constantly seeking to improve the way things are done

The role of leaders is to encourage people into an attitude which says, "If better is possible – good is not good enough".

Not only is this about learning from mistakes, it is also about learning from success. How often does the government appoint a public enquiry into things which go well? Not often? Why not; surely we have much to learn?

A useful approach is to adopt a Japanese technique called the 'Five whys'. This technique involves looking at results and asking 'Why?', then looking at the answer and asking 'Why?' again. Having done this five times we may be getting close to the nub of the issue and identifying what can be done to improve.

Summary checklist

✓ Consult and engage individuals in setting challenging targets for achievements and learning new approaches.

✓ Look for the current decisions you are 'putting off' and start the process that will lead to resolving them.

✓ Work out how to communicate your organisation's vision in a way people can relate to day by day.

7

Develops people and teams

> This chapter covers:
> > Emphasising learning.
> > Developing teamwork.
> > Dealing with breaches in standards.

One of the most important areas for achievement of leaders is in developing individuals and teams. This will be of huge importance in getting results for the organisation.

Key behaviours/attributes

The six behaviours here are:

- Encouraging other people to learn

- Encouraging people to work together as a team

- Regularly meeting with the team as a whole to review progress

- Taking time to develop and guide your staff

- Dealing effectively with breaches in standards of behaviour

- Treating other people's mistakes as learning opportunities.

Encouraging other people to learn

Much is spoken about the learning organisation, the knowledge economy and intellectual capital. What is clear is that the ability to learn and think ahead has now become as, or indeed more, important than experience.

Experience is extremely valuable – but more so in its relationship to people, self-awareness and development than to amassing knowledge. One of the problems with experience is that it can set limitations in our minds. Often the young new recruit to an organisation is of most value because 'they are too naïve to know it can't be done'.

This is not to say that older people or employees are less valuable. This is not about age, it is about outlook and approach. The increasing tendency towards a 'youth' culture has benefits, but it also has potential drawbacks as people get labelled, pigeon-holed or 'put out to grass'.

The most effective ways of learning are not simply trying to transfer knowledge and ideas from one person's head to another. As often they are about experiential learning or stepping into the unknown to try something out.

We can learn hugely both from results and from the process by which they were arrived at. A very simple technique which can be used for individuals, meetings or major projects is to ask:

- What went well?
- What went less well?
- What do we want to do/ see done differently next time?

Learning can be driven into the bloodstream not only by living the message but also by reinforcing it with recognition and reward via the performance appraisal system and organisational commitment to training and development.

Encouraging people to work together as a team

Most people recognise the benefits of teamwork, both in terms of the greater outputs realised through synergy and the human need for working with colleagues. Increasingly, teams are formed on a project or virtual basis rather than the traditional, fixed base 'departmental' type of team.

The leader's role specifically is to frame the team's goals and dependencies and to ensure people are clear about the shared values which influence how the team operates. Leaders will call regular meetings to discuss and share team progress and step in where blockages occur between individual members.

It is well to remember the classical stages associated with new or project teams:

- Forming (Cautious development – testing one another out)
- Storming (Openness, direct conversations, conflict)
- Norming (Settling into comfortable routines as trust builds)
- Performing (Being a high performing team).

At each of these stages, the leader is likely to need to act as a catalyst to see the team through to the next part of the cycle.

High performance teams are characterised by the leader who:

- Sets high expectations of output and behaviour
- Models good behaviours
- Speaks and lives an inspiring vision
- Gets people to live to their accountabilities and act responsibly on behalf of the whole team
- Deals with problem members
- Shares successes and learning in public.

Regularly meeting with the team as a whole to review progress

Building on the previous attribute, team meetings are one of the key ways to share, repeat and reinforce points about vision and direction, learning, progress and recognition.

It is always difficult to get busy people together and this can only be achieved with sensible drills and a requirement to attend. This does not override the need for individual one-to-ones, but does give the leader the opportunity to talk with the team face to face, gain immediate feedback and ensure everyone is at the same level of understanding on key issues.

Rotating the 'chairing' of meetings is a useful way of developing colleagues and ensuring continuity in the leader's absence. Do you pass the test of leadership that you can go on holiday, have no contact with the office and not come back to a raft of issues which could have been sorted by colleagues?

Taking time to develop and guide your staff

For the leader, effort spent here will pay huge dividends – as people develop, so performance will improve and the sense of satisfaction in seeing people grow is immense.

The word 'guide' is an important one as it places emphasis on the growing role of the leader as a coach. Coaching is about helping people to learn, not teaching, training or instructing. It is the essence of one-to-one development for the Liberating Leader.

A simple but effective approach is to use the 'GROW' model.
This means identifying:

Your	**G**OALS	(long and short term)
The current	**R**EALITY	of the situation
Your	**O**PTIONS	and alternatives
What	**W**ILL	you do?

To adopt this approach effectively requires questioning, reflecting back, summarising, generating feedback, use of silence, good appreciation of body language and application of 'active listening' techniques.

The scale and pace of change today means developing people is vital, including yourself as a leader. In order to progress we should, in a sense, all be trying to do ourselves out of our current job. Few people stay for ever in one organisation nowadays and the responsibility of leaders to ensure that people move on (internally or externally) with added value is both a moral duty and an organisational necessity.

Dealing effectively with breaches in standards of behaviour

This attribute is closely linked to taking unpopular decisions, and the same principles apply. The most important thing for leaders to do is to act early – the longer breaches apply, the greater the damage done and the more difficult it is to put things right.

Leaders need to act within procedure and with a view to bringing an individual up to standard. This includes ensuring that they understand what is required, that it is realistic and that they have the necessary resources and training to deliver. However, if all these positive steps are taken and improvement doesn't occur, then leaders need to be ready to dismiss people – this is never easy but it is not fair on the individual, their colleagues or 'customers' to be in a position they are clearly unsuited for.

The irony is that in command and control cultures discipline and breaches are more likely than in a liberated culture where people are treated more responsibly and act accordingly. In a liberated culture it is more likely that colleagues will support individuals and identify areas of poor performance; this aspect of positive peer pressure is an important distinction.

"At a meeting with a customer our supervisor found out that a member of his team had made an offer that was outside his remit. The supervisor took it on board quickly and showed the customer a better way of increasing his margin (with less cost to our company). Once outside he took the member of staff to task and warned him of his future conduct. The customer knew nothing of this".

Treating other people's mistakes as learning opportunities

It may sound a cliché to treat mistakes as learning opportunities, but like many clichés it has a solid grounding in reality.

Assuming the mistake is not wilful, slipshod, illegal, dangerous or frequently repeated, its occurrence, if handled well, can lead to a positive outcome.

The best process to adopt is to:

- Put right the mistake
- Review how it happened
- Agree action required to prevent reoccurrence.

Use of phrases such as "What are *we* going to do differently *next* time?" focuses on the action, sharing and future rather than becoming personalised and backward looking. We can't change what has happened and should concentrate on where we are right now.

Summary checklist

✓ Always review meetings, projects, successes and failures for what can be done next time to improve things.

✓ Promote team working through regular meetings, sharing information and project working.

✓ Deal with existing or future breaches in standards swiftly. They won't go away and if left untackled will undermine both your credibility as a leader and the effectiveness of your team.

8

Sets an example by their own behaviour

This chapter advises on:
> Setting an example.
> Being enthusiastic.
> Welcoming feedback.

Time and again during our research, respondents stated the importance of the leader 'living the message'. This is only likely consistently and genuinely to happen where a leader's *being* aligns with their *doing*. Many organisations have corporate vision statements on the wall in reception, but ultimately people will listen to what leaders do rather than what they say, and leaders in particular are scrutinised for how well they 'live the message'.

Key behaviours/attributes

The attributes within this area are:

- Actively encouraging feedback on your own performance
- Communicating an air of enthusiasm
- Working on your own learning

- Practising what you preach
- Openly admitting your mistakes
- Setting a good example to others by your own behaviour.

Actively encouraging feedback on your own performance

There is an old joke that we all welcome feedback, apart from that given by our partner, our children, our parents, our colleagues, etc. In truth, receiving feedback as opposed to acclaim is often emotionally tough, even though intellectually we know it to be right.

Feedback is valuable to everybody and leaders need to set an example by encouraging it as a normal part of working. Sometimes feedback can be requested at the end of a meeting, project or simply because you sense somebody is not happy.

The Industrial Society has developed a feedback tool called Liberating Leadership profiling based on the perceptions of the leader against the 38 behaviours.

Put simply, the leader rates themselves against the criteria and then asks five team members to do likewise, in confidence. This is not a psychometric or scientific test, it is a snapshot of how a set of team members *perceive* the leader based on their experience of the leader's behaviour. It may not be true but as their perception it is the team's *reality*. The aggregated results provide powerful messages and, more than anything, provide (if shared by the leader) the opportunity for dialogue based *not* around "Why did you score me in this way?", but "*What* would I need to do differently to increase the score?"

A vital first step to being a leader is to know oneself and feedback is an invaluable part of this. By setting an example and treating feedback as a 'gift' leaders are making a powerful statement about the open culture they wish to encourage.

Communicating an air of enthusiasm

Enthusiasm is infectious, as is lack of enthusiasm. For many people, overt displays of enthusiasm don't come easily! So, if you are naturally understated you may need as a leader to be yourself but with a bit of extra 'oomph'!

It is relatively easy to do this when things are new or going well, but less easy when things are not going well. But it is at these times that leadership really comes into play. The method here is not to dwell on the present and the negativity which may surround it, but to focus on the future and the actions required to move forward. This enables the leader to be positive and enthusiastic even if the current situation is dire.

Finally, choice of words and face-to-face communication are the way to really get enthusiasm across. After all, Martin Luther King in his greatest speech said, "I have a dream", not "I have a strategic plan".

Working on your own learning

Without this a leader will not only not succeed, they will not survive – such is the pace of change today. What is more, working on your own learning serves as a strong exemplar for colleagues.

As discussed earlier, experiential learning and reviewing learning 'on the job' are very powerful methods to go alongside reading, training, interactive learning, etc.

For leaders, the ability to be humble and show humility is important – they can learn a huge amount from people working in more junior roles within the organisation.

Practising what you preach

This is hugely important, and hugely difficult, because we are all human, and all fallible. But the impact that leaders' behaviour has on the team and organisation is massive – it is linked directly into integrity and therefore trust. This, as we have established, is the single most important underpinning for Liberating Leadership.

The difficulty for leaders is rarely that people take no notice of what they say, it is exactly the opposite. People take a great deal of notice of what you say AND WHAT YOU DO.

There is a story about a mother who brought her son to see Gandhi and said, "Please can you stop my son eating sugar". "Bring him back in two weeks", said Gandhi. In two weeks' time the mother returned and Gandhi said to the boy, "Stop eating sugar". The mother, curious, said, "Why did you not tell him two weeks ago?" Gandhi replied, "Two weeks ago I was eating sugar". Moral? Do as I do not as I say.

As Gandhi said, "We must *be* the change we wish to see in other people".

Openly admitting mistakes

My colleague, Christine Garner, once said in front of 70 deputy and head teachers, "I have never taken a wrong decision". The audience listened in disbelief until Christine explained, "I've never been presented with two options and thought option A looks right and option B looks wrong, and said I will go for option B. I have, however, frequently chosen option A to find out in retrospect that it was a bad choice".

This is a powerful image. Few of us wilfully make a mistake and it is important to consider the intent behind our actions, not just the result. Whereas there is often no need to jump in and make decisions quickly, where there is it is usually better to take the decision, own it and feel backed up than to prevaricate, defer or wait.

The power of the leader being open, explaining and sharing learning is immense.

Setting a good example to others by your own behaviour

Obvious examples of this are:

- Keeping to important standards and procedures (eg appraisal timetables, telephone answering standards, corporate lay-out of correspondence, etc).

- Role modelling new culture moves (eg removing status by the directors moving from reserved parking spaces to an 'equal access for all' policy; open plan offices, single status dining, etc are other instances.

- 'Griping up not down'. Staff want their boss to give reasons for management decisions, not to say "I agree it's typical of them upstairs". Leaders should do their complaining up the line but be positive down the line.

- Walking the job, using first names, genuinely listening to people.

If you as a leader face a difficult issue about how to behave, consider the following three rules of thumb:

- How would I like to be treated?

- How would this look on the front page of a national newspaper tomorrow?

- Could I explain my behaviour to my mother?

You may also ask your boss for 'three good reasons' why a decision has been taken if you are unhappy with 'selling' it on to your team.

"In a period of change, where little was known with any certainty about future jobs/career, [our] manager consistently made herself available for informal discussion, found out the latest information, ensured everyone knew. She also made a point of walking around and talking with people".

Summary checklist

✓ Adopt some form of feedback process on the perception of you as a leader and discuss the learning.

✓ 'Live' the messages you preach and treat it as a gift if colleagues point out inconsistencies in your role as leader – people will take great account of what you do (or don't do) rather than what you say.

9

Builds relationships based on trust

> This chapter considers:
> > Looking after other people's interests.
> > Keeping your word.
> > Being honest and fair.
> > Appearing calm.

You will recall that 'creating a climate of trusting relationships' was the most important theme from our research. It isn't hard to understand why. In this time of exponential change, leaders are rarely certain of anything more than a few months ahead. In asking people to move forward we are frequently saying we believe this to be the right direction or correct approach but we are not yet clear about *how* it will work. Colleagues will only be able to buy into this if they trust the intent of their leaders.

Key behaviours/attributes

There are seven behaviours in this area:

- Not putting self-interest before the interests of your staff

- Keeping promises and doing what you say you will do

- Being in touch with and sensitive to other people's feelings

- Being calm in a crisis and when under pressure
- Being honest and truthful
- Not taking personal credit for other people's work
- Always being fair.

Not putting self-interest before the interests of your staff

One of the main findings from our research was the inspiration followers draw from a leader who is prepared to consider their team's interests as well as their own. A Liberating Leader will gain a great deal of satisfaction from the success of their team. It is also likely that as team members' interests are looked after they will be more successful and have stronger feelings of support and personal loyalty to their leader.

Any leader who simply uses people to further their own ends is likely to be found out pretty quickly and not get the levels of engagement possible.

"I once worked for a line manager who, over a period of four years, led and built up a team in manufacturing and research which became the most successful in the company. On the break up of the company he helped all members of the team secure employment even though his own future was uncertain".

Keeping promises and doing what you say you will do

Real trust can only be built up over a period of time. We can act in the spirit of trusting somebody but it is really only verified by our experience of their behaviour and actions towards us over time.

Occasionally, a leader may find themselves in a position where their team or an individual team member feels they have not kept their promise – in such cases the leader should be upfront as early as possible about the reasons. In terms of judging their own people's behaviour, leaders also need to consider the *intent* behind people's actions, even a poor action motivated by good intent does not need to damage trust. As a leader you need to under-promise and over-deliver, never the other way round.

Being in touch with and sensitive to other people's feelings

Referring back to Daniel Goleman and emotional intelligence, you can see the importance of this approach. Real engagement and motivation comes from the heart not the head, and the heart is about feeling.

We talk about 'winning people's hearts and minds' – leadership is about both; but sensitivity and appeal to feelings is about the heart. In 1968 General Westmoreland, Commander US Forces in Vietnam, infamously said, "When you've got them by the balls, their hearts and minds will follow". The failure, despite massive military effort, to win that conflict points to the failure of the US to win the people's hearts in Vietnam.

In leadership terms, this sensitivity often comes more naturally to women – both for psychological and sociological reasons. The future may or may not be female, but there are a great many 'feminine' traits (eg listening, empathising, collegiate 'buy in') which managers of both sexes need to practise in order to become Liberating Leaders.

Being calm in a crisis and when under pressure

As enthusiasm rubs off so too can panic, and it is important that leaders don't convey this even if they may be feeling it inside.

A supervisor in our research was described as follows:

> *"When there's a crisis, other managers run around like headless chickens, but she's as cool as a cucumber. She uses the energy she saves for thinking".*

One way to stay calm is *not* to be rushed into a major decision. The late Lord Whitelaw, a former UK deputy Prime Minister, said when asked about the rumours of a date for the next election:

"There are decisions which have to be taken today, and decisions which don't have to be taken until tomorrow. I'm a great believer in not taking decisions which don't have to be taken today, today – or tomorrow."

Being honest and truthful

The value of this is self-evident. It does *not* mean spilling out everything in your thoughts ("Oh my God, your new haircut is awful!"), and as previously stated, there are areas where it is not appropriate to share. But it does require leaders to be genuine about what they discuss with their team, even and especially where it is unpalatable. It also requires the leader and the culture to move towards collaboration – open discussion with the relevant people rather than secret or corridor conversations.

Not taking personal credit for other people's work

Failure to do this is a quick and sure way to destroy trust. Recognition that team members need to support each other means credit needs to go where credit is due.

To some degree, Liberating Leaders miss out on the acclaim afforded traditional hierarchical managers where their sign-off, their job title and the existing expectation all combine to keep them in the limelight.

Liberating Leaders, by style and philosophy, will have a very 'hands off' approach – leading from within or behind as much as from the front. They need to realise that recognition will come from the success of the team and the growth of individuals within it.

"A manager of mine was a consistently good leader who listened well, coaxed ideas out of people, helped to formulate them and credited the originators with them".

Always being fair

Fairness covers a huge span of examples:

- Status and perks
- Personal favouritism
- Inconsistent behaviours
- Operation of codes and practices.

The best way for leaders to know if they are falling short is through feedback. If the right climate and processes are in place, this will be received pretty quickly and appropriate action can be taken. Another touchstone is to ask "How would I feel if I were on the receiving end?"

In cases where you, as a leader, are unsure it is useful to have a close confidant in or outside of the team – or to contact your mentor.

Summary checklist

✓ Keep a note of what you commit to and follow it through.

✓ Look for opportunities for other people to develop or receive credit and promote this.

✓ In a crisis, focus on the action to relieve the situation and move forward.

Any questions?

This chapter discusses:
> Are leaders born or made?
> Where do I start?
> Leadership/Personality style.
> What about my boss?

Key questions

1 Are leaders born or made?

The answer is likely to be *both*. Clearly we have different sets of abilities as individuals and these make it easier or harder to undertake certain leadership responsibilities. Our upbringing can also have a massive impact on our chances of becoming a good leader – whether our parents gave us confidence, whether they are in a position to offer opportunities and networks, etc.

However, personal commitment, development, learning and aspiration can overcome most barriers, or indeed waste many opportunities. Thankfully, society is changing and whereas the old school tie, gender, race, age, etc still influence many people, there is no doubt that we are moving towards a more open, meritocratic society where relationships are based on trust, shared values and achievement rather than position or background.

2 What should I do as a leader now?

Start now!

Fundamentally, you must start to *live* the culture and organisation we wish to have – NOW. As leader you are both part of the problem and part of the solution. If you believe in trust you must trust people, if you believe in removing status markers and procedures you must do so.

You have to begin with yourself and being true to your beliefs. It is amazing what impact one person can have – but when you consider the number of interactions you have as a leader, or simply as an individual, in a day or a month, perhaps it is not so surprising. (The so-called "moments of truth" as expressed by Jan Carlsson of SAS Airlines.)

Welcome feedback

Get 180° or 360° feedback from your team, colleagues, suppliers and boss. The key to encouraging feedback is to demonstrate a commitment to the principle by doing it, and then create the possibility for discussions about how to improve your performance as a leader. A questionnaire which provides a snapshot view at individual, managerial or organisational level is at the end of the book (see Appendix 2, p. 83).

You can make receiving feedback a normal part of your working style by:

- Quick reviews after meetings/projects/one-to-ones – what went well, what went less well, how you could improve

- Having one or more trusted colleagues who can really give it to you straight, or with whom you can share your inner-most thoughts.

Get a mentor

A mentor is a senior, trusted person whom you can have confidential discussions with and who can advise, guide or act as a sounding board. Get yourself a mentor, inside or outside the organisation – preferably both.

Learn and observe

Watch other leaders and see what works, and what doesn't, and then try it yourself. Keep up your reading and attend workshops, sessions or training every so often to "sharpen your saw" as Stephen Covey put it in his best-selling book *The 7 Habits of Highly Effective People*.

Sort out your vision/values

Decide what you are trying to achieve as a leader, what values are key to you and how you are going to reflect these in your behaviour.

By doing this you can begin to see how far you are 'living your life' whilst you are at work.

3 Do I need to be charismatic?

Charisma can of course help, but it really is in the eye of the beholder and there are many different forms. The classic 'white charger' leadership does not always liberate people and almost always leads to a vacuum when the leader moves on. There are a great many good leaders in the world – if charisma was essential you would literally keep bumping into such people, and you don't!

4 Do I need to be forceful?

If by forceful you mean aggressive – NO! Aggression will get movement and therefore results, but it will not get engagement and therefore misses out on what is possible, building up resentment for the future. If by forceful you mean assertive – YES!

Fundamental to assertiveness is going for a win/win result. There really is no such thing as a win/lose as the 'loser' will always get their own back, even if only by withholding a part of their efforts. It does not mean compromise either but seeking to find the key to a success on the other person's or people's terms as well as your own.

5 What if my boss/organisation doesn't behave in a liberated way?

This is a common refrain, sometimes real, often an excuse for inactivity. Of course, there may be some structural and procedural limitations, but the impact you as a leader can have on your team and their performance, on colleagues and as a role model, can be significant. Concentrate on the things you *can* affect (your circle of influence) rather than those you can't (circle of concern) – that way you achieve more, feel more positive and increase the zone of influence.

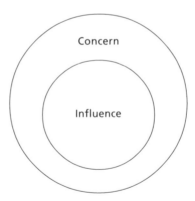

You can also work at changing systems and culture formally by piloting new methods, systems, etc – in which case either just do it and keep your boss informed or make the case and seek approval.

Providing you make a case which can show potential benefits in line with the boss's agenda it will have a good chance of going ahead.

6 Does leadership style need to alter as you become more senior?

Fundamentally the basic approach remains the same. The main difference is about closeness to the job and attention to detail. More senior leaders spend less time 'doing the now' and more 'being' and thinking of the future. Such people will be scrutinised by staff for whether they 'walk the talk' and the grapevine will do the rest. It is very easy to lose touch with the organisation so clear drills for holding staff updates and walking the job become vital. Diarying ahead, using 'bring forward' systems for birthdays, keeping a note of personal facts (kids' names, etc) and being well briefed on local issues and personnel by middle managers are all important.

Summary checklist

- ✓ Find the right approval for the leader within you.
- ✓ Get some form of feedback from those you lead.
- ✓ Identify your own action plan to improve as a leader and gain one or more mentors/supporters/colleagues to help you on the journey.
- ✓ Focus on what you *can* influence, don't get bogged down worrying about what you can't.

Leadership in the future

Our concept of leadership

We need to alter our concept of leadership in response to three key questions.

1 Who will be leaders?

"We are all leaders now" was a statement I heard from Richard Field, Chairman Dyson Refractories plc, some years back. I firmly believe he was right. Not that we are all managers.

As organisations flatten, increase their responsiveness to customers and to change, set up and disband project teams, work with associate 'knowledge workers', etc, so the scope for practising leadership broadens and the need increases. Leaders are not just at the top of organisations, not just managers – but anyone involved in a situation where leadership skills and behaviours need to be put to work. On this point I am hugely optimistic because when you scratch the surface of people's activities – especially beyond work – you realise that there is no 'crisis' of leadership, merely an under-utilisation of a reservoir of talent.

2 What style is required?

The main message is that we must move on from the restrictive concept of the 'white charger' leader. Always out in front, often charismatic – frequently male and military! Not to say this style was wrong, simply that it was a product of its age and circumstances. Some of these traits *are* required at times but consider the potential drawbacks to such an approach:

- It is personality dependent
- It can result in people mistakenly following leaders
- It frequently fails to leave a thriving legacy for successors.

Leaders for the future will lead as often from within or behind as from the front. They will be *followers* as well as leaders (see Appendix 1, p. 81)

The climate they create and the journey they take will be as important as the result. It is not good enough to say the "end justifies the means" if we abandon all our principles and humanity in the process. Such issues must be carefully considered.

3 How will good leadership be judged?

By considering the following areas:

- Achievement of results (Destination)
- Method of achievement (Journey)
- Legacy (Is it long lasting and positive?)
- Adding value (Have the followers and successors grown as a result and are they able to take forward the organisation in the future?).

Conclusion

Leadership is the vital catalyst for successful change whether it be individually, in a team, for an organisation or in the wider community.

As we start the 21st century we have a unique opportunity and a great responsibilty as individual leaders to shape the future we wish to see rather than be slaves to it.

I hope that this book has helped to provide insights around the mix of strategy and tactics, 'being' and 'doing', hands on and hands off, that is needed to develop ourselves as leaders.

All our futures are dependent on it.

Appendix 1

Liberating Leaders v Traditional Leaders	
LIBERATING LEADERS	TRADITIONAL LEADERS
∅ Achieve success in leaps and bounds	∅ Achieve incremental improvements
∅ Are people/team focused	∅ Are driven by status and financial gain
∅ Embody the highest ethical standards	∅ Accept and exemplify double standards
∅ Are role models, living the beliefs and values they put forward in order to reinforce the trust they need	∅ Use leadership jargon but don't practise what they preach
∅ Act based on the long-term common interest	∅ Are short-termist and self-interested
∅ Allow people the freedom to test things out in a way that suits them	∅ Restrict the ability of others to develop by imposing too much control and structure
∅ Communicate and share an inspiring vision of the future	∅ Focus only on tactical issues
∅ Respect every individual's ability to show leadership in all areas, at all levels of our communities and organisations	∅ Don't support individuals who want to take responsibility for leading differently and in a broader context

Appendix 2

Achieving results by building trust

Research conducted by The Industrial Society has established a strong link between leadership and encouraging a climate of trust. The questionnaire below is designed to give you a quick insight into the degree of trust between people in your organisation.

	Not at all	To a small extent	To a modest extent	To a great extent	To a very great extent
How satisfied are you that:					
• Systems and procedures encourage 'ownership' and are based on presumption of trust and competence?	1	2	3	4	5
• The organisation treats employees, suppliers and customers fairly and ethically?	1	2	3	4	5
• Mistakes are seen as learning opportunities, rather than a chance to apportion blame?	1	2	3	4	5
• People willingly contribute their ideas knowing they are welcome and that they will receive credit for them?	1	2	3	4	5

	Not at all	To a small extent	To a modest extent	To a great extent	To a very great extent
How satisfied are you that:					
• People who do the work make decisions about how the work is done and use their discretion to make improvements?	1	2	3	4	5
• Communication is open – people know and understand data relating to team and organisation performance?	1	2	3	4	5
• The organisation generally cares for its employees?	1	2	3	4	5
• Managers practise what they preach?	1	2	3	4	5

Interpreting your score

30 – 40   Your managers are doing the right things and are generally respected by their staff.

20 – 30   Your managers demonstrate some of the behaviours which build positive, trusting relationships but do not fully realise employees' potential.

10 – 20   Relationships and results could be improved significantly.

0 – 10   Oh dear ! Your organisation is based on mutual suspicion. There is much work to be done.